warriors @work

what the smartest business
leaders are saying

FranklinCovey.

Other Books from Franklin Covey

What Counts: How Forward-Thinking Leaders Recognize and Reward Employees
The 7 Habits of Highly Effective People
The 7 Habits of Highly Effective Families
The 7 Habits of Highly Effective Teens
The 7 Habits of Highly Effective Teens Journal
Daily Reflections for Highly Effective People
Living the 7 Habits
Choice: Choosing the Proactive Life You Want to Live
Renewal: Nourishing Heart, Mind, Body, and Soul
Loving Reminders for Kids
Loving Reminders for Couples
Loving Reminders for Families
Loving Reminders Teen to Teen
Quotes and Quips

Franklin Covey
2200 West Parkway Boulevard
Salt Lake City, Utah 84119-2099

Concept by Cheryl Kerzner
Written and compiled by Debra Harris
Book design by David Volsic
Manufactured in United States of America
ISBN 1-929494-08-4

ABILITY

AMBITION

ATTITUDE

CHALLENGE

GROWTH

INNOVATION

LEADERSHIP

MOTIVATION

PURPOSE

SUCCESS

INTRODUCTION

The most exciting breakthrough of the
21st century will occur not because of technology,
but because of an expanding concept of what
it means to be human.

JOHN NAISBETT, *MEGATRENDS 2000*

In **Warriors@Work: What the Smartest Business Leaders Are Saying**, you'll discover a right-up-to-the-minute compilation of powerful sound bites, intelligent insights, and clever quips on the new world of business for the new millennium. This collection of contemporary quotes was accumulated from the world's best and brightest business visionaries with one purpose in mind: to help motivate you to find your own brand of leadership as well as inspire those around you to develop their own qualities for success. Snapped from the most forward-thinking business magazines, articles, books, interviews, and other business and online sources, these powerful comments give you practical tools and advice that will impact your life now and in the future.

From such visionaries as Bill Gates, Warren Bennis, Anita Roddick, Faith Popcorn, Peter Drucker, Howard Schultz, and Rosabeth Moss Kanter to the most innovative thinkers Silicon Valley has to offer, these words are insightful, straight to the point, funny, poignant, and often biting. But always thought-provoking and impactive to help you stretch your boundaries, think outside the box, challenge your ideas, and allow yourself to dream even bigger dreams.

For anyone in a management position or who has the burning desire to succeed, **Warriors@Work** is a must-read, a must-repeat, and a must-share over and over again.

ABILITY

I don't expect anyone to be perfect. It's not

HUMAN NATURE

What I do expect is that you will take risks, correct mistakes, and learn from both. And if you don't—judging by market results—then we'll make a change. It's nothing personal. And I'll do it, even if you're my best friend. We must have this company execute to its full potential.

MIKE ARMSTRONG, CEO, AT&T

to be a manager,
    you have to start at the bottom
     —no exceptions.

HENRY BLOCK, CEO, H&R BLOCK

There was a time when I thought brains were everything. That view has dimmed recently. I think brains are important, but now I also look for a lot of collateral assets. I look for people who are team-builders, good communicators, courageous people who don't get stuck with an idea. You need people who are more nimble, who have the ability to lead organizations in changing and tumultuous times comfortably, without panicking. That doesn't mean you sacrifice your principles, but it sure means you take a second look at issues and topics. You might have a different view in a year than you do now.

LARRY BOSSIDY, CEO, ALLIEDSIGNAL

In the business world, everyone is paid in two coins: cash and experience. Take the experience first; the cash comes later.

HAROLD GENEEN, CEO, IT&T

I'll pay more for a man's ability to express himself than for any other quality he might possess.

CHARLES SCHWAB, CEO, CHARLES SCHWAB

to love what you do
and feel that it matters,
how could anything be more
fun?

if you can run one
business well,
you can run any
business well.

RICHARD BRANSON, FOUNDER AND CHAIRMAN, THE VIRGIN GROUP

Never allow your sense of self to become associated with your sense of job. If your job vanishes, your self doesn't.

GORDEN VAN SAUTER, FORMER PRESIDENT, CBS NEWS

Beware of a misfit occupation...Consider carefully your natural bent, whether for business or a profession.

MARSHALL FIELD, FOUNDER, MARSHALL FIELD

I ask people, "What are you good at?" It's remarkable the number of people that don't speak to that question with any degree of insight. You've got to know what you're good at. I've been lucky; I can make things happen. I can get the people to identify with what we want to do, and I can get it done. You've got to know what you're good at because those are the cards you bring to the party. In other words, you need a sense of who you are and where you are going in order to be a successful manager.

LARRY BOSSIDY, CEO, ALLIEDSIGNAL

you only have to
do a few things right
in your life so long as you don't
do too many things wrong.

WARREN BUFFETT, INVESTOR, CEO, BERKSHIRE HATHAWAY

Deals are my art form.

Other people paint beautifully on canvas or write wonderful poetry.

I like making deals, preferably big deals. That's how I get my kicks.

DONALD TRUMP, PRESIDENT, TRUMP ORGANIZATION

We spend January first walking through our lives, room by room, drawing up a list of work to be done, cracks to be patched. Maybe this year, to balance the list, we ought to walk through the rooms of our lives...not looking for flaws, but for potential.

ELLEN GOODMAN, COLUMNIST

there is something that is much more
scarce, something rarer than ability. it is
the ability to recognize ability.

ROBERT HALF, PERSONNEL AGENCY EXECUTIVE

ability

will never catch up
with the demand for it.

MALCOLM FORBES, PUBLISHER, *FORBES*

Put yourself in a state of mind where you say to yourself, "Here is an opportunity for me to celebrate like never before, my own power, my own ability to get myself to do whatever is necessary."

ANTHONY ROBBINS, MOTIVATIONAL SPEAKER AND AUTHOR

you

are the only person on earth

who can use your ability.

ZIG ZIGLAR, MOTIVATIONAL SPEAKER AND AUTHOR

once you think
you can write down
what made you successful,
you won't be.

LOU GERSTNER, CHAIRMAN AND CEO, IBM

AMBITION

If you want to be a

WORLD-CLASS PERFORMER

and I don't want to have anybody with me who doesn't dream of that, then you're not going to set goals that are easy to achieve. You won't do that because you wouldn't be able to live with yourself. You would not be worth knowing.

DAVID JOHNSON, CHAIRMAN, CAMPBELL SOUP

As you enter positions of trust and power, dream a little before you think.

TONI MORRISON, AUTHOR

We know only two things about the future: It cannot be known, and it will be different from what exists now and from what we now expect.

PETER DRUCKER, BUSINESS PHILOSOPHER AND AUTHOR

you can deal with the future
more clearly if you don't
focus on the next week.

JOHN TEMPLETON, FOUNDER, TEMPLETON FUNDS

there's a lot
one person can do.

DENNIS KOZLOWSKI, CHAIRMAN, TYCO

when in doubt, make a fool of yourself. there is a microscopically thin line between being brilliantly creative and acting like the most gigantic idiot on earth...leap!

CYNTHIA HEIMEL, AUTHOR

What I wanted

was to be allowed to do the thing in the world that I did best, which I believed then and believe now, is the greatest privilege there is. when I did that success found me.

A man to carry on a successful business must have imagination.

He must see things as in a vision, a dream of the whole thing.

CHARLES SCHWAB, CEO, CHARLES SCHWAB

if you have a job without aggravations,
you don't have a job.

MALCOLM FORBES, PUBLISHER, *FORBES*

What if Columbus had been told, "Chris, baby, don't go now. Wait until we've solved our number-one priorities: war and famine; poverty and crime; pollution and disease; illiteracy and racial hatred?..."

BILL GATES, FOUNDER, CHAIRMAN, AND CEO, MICROSOFT

don't be **against things** so much as **for things.**

COLONEL HARLAND SANDERS, FOUNDER, KENTUCKY FRIED CHICKEN

Apply yourself. Get all the education you can, but then, by God,

do something. Don't just stand there, make it happen.

LEE IACOCCA, FORMER CHAIRMAN, CHRYSLER

You have to have passion, and that passion has to come through. I'll take a smart person with passion over someone with years of experience any day. People with intelligence and passion will get the problem solved, no matter what.

CAROL BARTZ, CEO, AUTODESK

don't spend time
beating on a wall,
hoping to transform it into a door.

LAURA SCHLESSINGER, RADIO TALK SHOW HOST

Life is the movie you see through your own eyes. it makes little difference what's happening out there. it's how you take it that counts.

DENIS WAITLEY, MOTIVATIONAL SPEAKER AND AUTHOR

you do not have to be

superhuman

to do what you believe in.

DEBBI FIELDS, FOUNDER, MRS. FIELDS' COOKIES

ATTITUDE

I have the most

FUN JOB IN THE WORLD

and love coming to work each day because there are always

new opportunities, and new thing to learn. If you enjoy your job

this much, you will never burn out.

BILL GATES, FOUNDER, CHAIRMAN, AND CEO, MICROSOFT

What advice would I give my grandchildren? That's the easiest question in the world. Do something you enjoy—music, business, public service, whatever. If they don't care if their IQ is 30 points higher, the guy with the inferior IQ—who loves what he is doing—will beat them to death.

ACE GREENBERG, CHAIRMAN, BEAR STEARNS

I'd rather be lucky than smart.

DON FISHER, FOUNDER AND CHAIRMAN, GAP

the first rule is
write your own rules.

FAST COMPANY

I've always felt that you shouldn't have to change your personality when you come to work. So we decided we are going to hire good people, and let them be themselves, let them be individualistic. We were going to create an environment where we pay a great deal of attention to them, their personal lives as well as their business lives. We wanted to show them that we don't regard them just as work automatons. We wanted to create an environment where people can really enjoy what they are doing.

HERB KELLEHER, FOUNDER, CHAIRMAN, AND CEO, SOUTHWEST AIRLINES

there's nothing in the

middle of
the road

but yellow stripes and

dead armadillos.

JIM HIGHTOWER, TEXAS AGRICULTURAL COMMISSIONER

When you're in your nineties and looking back, it's not going to be how much money you made or how many awards you've won. It's really what did you stand for. Did you make a positive difference for people?

ELIZABETH DOLE, FORMER U.S. SECRETARY OF TRANSPORTATION
AND AMERICAN RED CROSS EXECUTIVE

The individual is forcing the change. People are shopping around, not only for the right job but for the right atmosphere. They now regard the old rules of business as dishonest, boring, and outdated. This new generation in the workplace is saying "I want a society and a job that values me more than the gross national product. I want work that engages the heart as well as the mind and the body, that fosters friendship and that nourishes the earth. I want to work for a company that contributes to the community."

ANITA RODDICK, FOUNDER, BODY SHOP

The moment you commit and quit holding back, all sorts of unforeseen incidents, meetings and material assistance will rise up to help you. The simple act of commitment is a powerful magnet for help.

NAPOLEON HILL, AUTHOR, *THINK AND GROW RICH*

those who enjoy responsibility
usually get it;
those who merely like exercising
authority usually lose it.

MALCOLM FORBES, PUBLISHER, *FORBES*

think people's egos are a big problem in running a business. I haven't let my own ego get in the way. I'd just as soon have other people get credit for good results rather than me. If I were to take credit for all of it, it would be very discouraging to the person who really did the work. You've got to respect the other person's ideas as well. There's no reason not to fight for your ideas, if you think you're right. But if the other person's idea is better, you should accept it and then be a big supporter of it. This is something many people—especially newly minted MBAs—fail to understand.

DON FISHER, FOUNDER AND CHAIRMAN, GAP

you can either **take action**
or you can hang back and hope for a miracle.
miracles are great, but they are so
unpredictable.

PETER DRUCKER, BUSINESS PHILOSOPHER AND AUTHOR

it's a good idea not to major in minor things.

ANTHONY ROBBINS, MOTIVATIONAL SPEAKER AND AUTHOR

Nothing splendid

has ever been achieved except by those who dared believe that something inside them was superior to circumstances.

BRUCE BARTON, ADVERTISING EXECUTIVE AND AUTHOR

Never look at the doors closing behind you or you'll miss the ones opening ahead.

CYRIL MAGNIN, CHAIR, JOSEPH MAGNIN

I've begun to realize that I can't have it all. I used to think that I could if I scheduled artfully enough. But you have to make choices.

JOY COVEY, CHIEF STRATEGY OFFICER, AMAZON.COM

The first thing I always say is that within reason, you can accomplish almost everything in life that you want to, as long as you're willing to work hard—and smart—to get it. The second is deal with life the way it is, not the way you wish it was, and if you have hurdles thrown in front of you, learn how to get over them, rather than let them distract you. Third, you really should treat people the way you would like to be treated yourself. The last element? Have fun. Don't take life too seriously.

JOHN CHAMBERS, CEO, CISCO SYSTEMS

CHALLENGE

All you can do is the best you can. Stay on the

BALLS OF YOUR FEET

as you might in a tennis game. Be ready to change directions if you need to, but don't do it in haste (as one might have to in tennis), and above all, worry about your customers. Customers can go away in a drop of a hat.

MARTHA INGRAM, CHAIRMAN AND CEO, INGRAM INDUSTRIES

I've been harassed,
called a bimbo,
and told time
and time again
I couldn't do something.
I didn't believe it.

CARLY FIORINA, CEO, HEWLETT-PACKARD

A successful man is one who can lay a firm foundation with the bricks that others throw at him.

DAVID BRINKLEY, TELEVISION NEWS ANCHOR

often you have to rely on your intuition.

BILL GATES, FOUNDER, CHAIRMAN, AND CEO, MICROSOFT

it never pays to deal with the flyweights of the world. they take far too much pleasure in thwarting you at every turn.

SUE GRAFTON, AUTHOR

Always continue the climb. It is possible for you to do whatever you choose, if you first get to know who you are and are willing to work with a power that is greater than ourselves to do it.

OPRAH WINFREY, CHAIRMAN, HARPO ENTERTAINMENT

I wanted to be scared again...
I wanted to feel unsure again.
That's the only way I learn,
the only way I feel challenged.

CONNIE CHUNG, TELEVISION NEWS ANCHOR

Invariably, the mistakes you look back on with regret involve situations where you played it too safe. In our case, we decided for a period of time to follow instead of lead. As a consequence, we fell back into mimicking and reacting to what others were doing instead of deciding that leadership was the way we needed to go.

MIKE VOLKEMA, PRESIDENT AND CEO, HERMAN MILLER

just before consumers stop doing something,
they do it with a **vengeance.**

FAITH POPCORN, FOUNDER, BRAINRESERVE, AND AUTHOR

take risks.
you can't fall off the bottom.

BARBARA PROCTOR, ADVERTISING EXECUTIVE

one of the most feared

expressions in modern times is

"the computer is down."

NORMAN AUGUSTINE, CHAIRMAN, MARTIN MARIETTA

assumption
is the mother of
screw-up.

ANGELO DONGHIA, INTERIOR DESIGNER

Hire the best. Pay them fairly. Communicate frequently. Provide challenges and rewards. Believe in them. Get out of their way and they'll knock your socks off.

MARY ANN ALLISON, VICE PRESIDENT, CITICORP

GROWTH

If you really believe what you're doing is right, and you

BELIEVE IT'S IMPORTANT

and you truly feel that you are a pioneer who is making a difference, you may make some mistakes, but your energy and commitment will help you overcome them. The perseverance is important particularly in new industries because there are many times where the so-called smart thing may be to throw up your hands and quit because it's hard, or you've hit a brick wall. But you have to think "Well, we're just going to keep at it. That is critical."

STEVE CASE, COFOUNDER, CHAIRMAN, AND CEO, AMERICA ONLINE

in a start-up company, you basically
throw out all assumptions
every three weeks.

SCOTT MCNEALY, CEO, SUN MICROSYSTEMS

No one ever won a chess game by betting on each move.

Sometimes you have to move backward to get a step forward.

AMAR BOSE, CEO, BOSE

the revolution is going to happen. it's just a matter of whether you're with it or you're behind it.

FAST COMPANY

59

Are you green and growing
or ripe and rotting?

RAY KROC, FOUNDER, MCDONALD'S

We are constantly challenging what we do—building a culture of restless self-renewal.

LOU GERSTNER, CHAIRMAN AND CEO, IBM

when you're through changing, you're through.

BRUCE BARTON, ADVERTISING EXECUTIVE AND AUTHOR

usually if everybody

is going in one direction

it's wrong.

HANK GREENBERG, CHAIRMAN AND CEO, AMERICAN INTERNATIONAL

Holding people accountable helps them grow. People want to know if they haven't done a good job and how they can do better. It helps them to be measured against appropriate norms or standards. Our responsibility is to encourage and drive them to achieve, and help them where they fall short, so they can ultimately succeed. That kind of toughness is very important to our organization's morale and ultimately to our performance.

CHUCK KNIGHT, CHAIRMAN, EMERSON ELECTRIC

Living systems are drawn to the edge of chaos because that is where the capacity for information processing and learning—therefore, growth—is maximized.

DEE HOCK, FOUNDER, VISA

to grow faster than one is able to manage is flirting with disaster.

AN WANG, FOUNDER, WANG

In the best people I see a commitment to a continual learning. I don't mean education, necessarily, in a formal way, but they are people who are constantly in search of new information and new ways they can integrate it into a framework that they carry around in their head. In other words, they never become complacent.

PAUL O'NEILL, CHAIRMAN AND CEO, ALCOA

Don't be embarrassed by your achievements. Being an overachiever is nothing despicable. It is only admirable. Never lower your standards.

MARTHA STEWART, FOUNDER, MARTHA STEWART LIVING OMNIMEDIA

trust is the lubrication that makes it possible for organizations to work.

WARREN BENNIS, LEADERSHIP EDUCATOR, SPEAKER, AND AUTHOR

I will grow.

I will become something new and grand, but no grander than I now am. Just as the sky will be different in a few hours, its present perfection and completeness is not deficient, so am I presently perfect and not deficient because I will be different tomorrow. I will grow, and I am not deficient.

WAYNE DYER, MOTIVATIONAL SPEAKER AND AUTHOR

If it's not growing, it's going to die.

MICHAEL EISNER, CEO, WALT DISNEY PRODUCTIONS

The most important trait of a good leader is knowing who you are. In our industry, very often we don't have time to think. You have to do all your homework, but then you have to go with your intuition without letting your mind get in the way. We all have a fantasy that we control what happens to us in our lives—and this is especially true of CEOs. But in fact none of us have that kind of control. Meditation helps me with that, giving me more confidence that I can let go of the feeling that I have to control everything and things will still turn out all right.

ED MCCRACKEN, CEO, SILICON GRAPHICS

INNOVATION

Everyone who's ever

TAKEN A SHOWER

has an idea. It's the person who gets out of the shower, dries

off and does something about it who makes a difference.

NOLAN BUSHNELL, FOUNDER, ATARI

never kill an idea, just deflect it.

3M COMPANY

The key to building an enduring

new medium

is passion, people, perseverance,

perspective, and paranoia.

STEVE CASE, COFOUNDER, CHAIRMAN, AND CEO, AMERICA ONLINE

The creative person wants to be a know-it-all. He wants to know about all kinds of things: ancient history, nineteenth century mathematics, current manufacturing techniques, flower arranging, and hog futures. Because he never knows when these ideas might come together to form a new idea. It may happen six minutes later or six months down the road. But he has faith that it will happen.

CARL ALLY, FOUNDER, ALLY & GARGANO ADVERTISING

The thing that will separate you from everyone else is a combination of innovativeness, creativity, and self-motivation. Some people need to be told all the time what to do, and if that describes you, that's okay. We'll give you lots of direction. But the people who are going to stand out are those who take the initiative and are self-motivated to anticipate how they can be supportive. They will be recognized for reaching down and helping, mentoring, and developing people.

WALTER SHIPLEY, CHAIRMAN, CHASE MANHATTAN

great teams

are not hierarchical or autocratic; they tap each member's creative potential.

FAST COMPANY

A new idea is delicate. It can be killed by a sneer or a yawn; it can be stabbed to death by a joke or worried to death by a frown on the right person's brow.

CHARLES BROWER, PRESIDENT,
BATTEN, BARTON, DURSTINE & OSBORNE ADVERTISING

The cost of perfection will drive you out of business. What you are striving for is magic, not perfection.

MICHAEL EISNER, CHAIRMAN AND CEO, WALT DISNEY PRODUCTIONS

Most people are more comfortable with old problems than with new solutions.

ANONYMOUS

Don't fear failure so much that you refuse to try new things. The saddest summary of a life contains three descriptions: could have, might have, and should have.

LOUIS E. BOONE, EDUCATOR AND BUSINESS WRITER

if you do things well,
do them better. be daring,
be first,
be different, be just.

ANITA RODDICK, FOUNDER, BODY SHOP

When nighttime comes, the competition plots while we sleep. Therefore, we're going to have people working around the clock and it's not just going to be the fact that they are working that matters, it is the quality of the work and their inventiveness that's important, otherwise you can quickly be outmaneuvered.

DAVID JOHNSON, CHAIRMAN, CAMPBELL SOUP

Do not fear

to be eccentric in opinion, for every opinion

now accepted was once eccentric.

BERTRAND RUSSELL, PHILOSOPHER

implementers aren't considered bozos anymore.

JOHN SCULLEY, CHAIRMAN, APPLE COMPUTER

Rules for Stifling Innovation

Regard any new idea from below with suspicion—because it's new, and because it's from below.

Insist that people who need your approval to act first go through several other levels of management to get their signatures.

Ask departments or individuals to challenge and criticize each other's proposals. (That saves you the job of deciding; you just pick the survivor.)

And above all, never forget that you, the high-ups, already know everything important about this business.

ROSABETH MOSS KANTER, HARVARD BUSINESS SCHOOL PROFESSOR AND AUTHOR

doing business on the Internet has forced me to unlearn everything I knew about anything.

ANDREW PARKINSON, PRESIDENT AND CEO, PEAPOD

Failure is just another way to learn how to do something right.

MARIAN WRIGHT EDELMAN, PRESIDENT, CHILDREN'S DEFENSE FUND

LEADERSHIP

It's very difficult to lead today when people are not really

PARTICIPATING

in the decision. You won't be able to attract and retain great people if they don't feel like they are a part of the authorship of the strategy and the authorship of really critical issues. If you don't give people an opportunity to really be engaged, they won't stay.

HOWARD SCHULTZ, CHAIRMAN AND CEO, STARBUCKS

ere is the very heart and soul of the matter: If you look to lead, invest at least 40% of your time managing yourself—your ethics, character, principle, purpose, motivation, and conduct. Invest at least 30% managing those with authority over you, and 15% managing your peers. Use the remainder to induce those you "work for" to understand and practice the theory...if you don't understand that you should be working for your mislabeled "subordinates" you haven't understood anything. Lead yourself, lead your superiors, lead your peers, and free your people to do the same. All else is trivial.

DEE HOCK, FOUNDER, VISA

One of the biggest things I've learned
is that I don't always have to be right.

even leaders
are led.

A leadership skill that inspires confidence and trust can be expressed in a variety of ways. It doesn't have to be charismatic. It can be pretty low key. But it has to be there.

RAY GILMARTIN, CHAIRMAN, PRESIDENT, AND CEO, MERCK

today, a great CEO must be a great communicator.

FRED RAINES, CEO, FEDEX

I don't believe a CEO should be living in some kind of an ivory tower thinking great thoughts. I believe in a hands-on management approach. You've got to be out there doing it.

HANK GREENBERG, CHAIRMAN AND CEO, AMERICAN INTERNATIONAL

A leader is someone
who can take a group of
people to a place they
don't think they can go.

BOB EATON, CHAIRMAN AND CO-CEO, DAIMLERCHRYSLER

Organizations need to have someone at the top who can keep everybody on track, and who will determine whether a particular item being discussed is part of its focus or not. People lose track of what the goal is after a while. They start to get caught up in doing the day to day things and forget what you were ultimately trying to do as an enterprise.

FRANK RAINES, CHAIRMAN AND CEO, FANNIE MAE

The way to be a leader today is different. I no longer call the shots. I'm not the decision maker. The essence of leadership today is to make sure that the organization knows itself.

MORT MEYERSON, CHAIRMAN AND CEO, PEROT SYSTEMS

be willing to make decisions.

that's the most important quality in a good leader. don't fall victim to what I call the "ready-aim-aim-aim syndrome." you must be willing to fire.

T. BOONE PICKENS, FOUNDER, UNITED SHAREHOLDERS

I've learned that my role is less about what I can do and more about what the organization can do.

JASON OLIM, PRESIDENT AND CEO, CDNOW

For the persuasive power of leadership to be really effective, the organization needs this goal, a dream that the institution is living out and that the leadership is serving. It is not the "I" or the ultimate leader that moves an institution to greatness, but the dream. We are all subordinates to the great idea.

MARK SHEPARD, FORMER CHAIRMAN, TEXAS INSTRUMENTS

Good business leaders create a vision, articulate the vision, passionately own the vision, and relentlessly drive it to completion.

JOHN WELCH, CEO, GENERAL ELECTRIC

The job of the manager is enabling, not a directive job...coaching and not direction is the first quality of leadership now. Get the barriers out of the way to let people do the things they do well.

ROBERT NOYCE, FOUNDER, INTEL

A leader has the vision and conviction that a dream can be achieved. He inspires the power and energy to get it done.

RALPH LAUREN, FASHION DESIGNER

Managers do things right.
Leaders do the right things.

WARREN BENNIS AND BURT NANUS, LEADERSHIP EDUCATORS AND AUTHORS

are you waiting for someone

to lead and inspire you

for the boss to recognize you

for clients to thank you

for coworkers to help you

for the world to hail you

well here's a news flash

they are all just sitting there too

waiting for you.

boss creates fear, a leader confidence. A boss fixes blame, a leader corrects mistakes. A boss knows all, a leader asks questions. A boss makes work drudgery, a leader makes it interesting. A boss is interested in himself or herself; a leader is interested in the group.

RUSSELL H. EWING, PRESIDENT, NATIONAL INSTITUTE FOR LEADERSHIP

As long as we operate within this old paradigm we are separated from our heart and values and feel powerless. We cannot suspend our values during the workday and think we will have them when we get home. We're all interconnected.

There is a spiritual dimension to business just as to individuals.

BEN COHEN AND JERRY GREENFIELD, FOUNDERS, BEN & JERRY'S ICE CREAM

MOTIVATION

You have to

COMMIT TO VALUES

as you generate both personal and organizational energy. You have to create excitement as well as opportunity. We spend so much time working; it's got to be fun as well as rewarding for people. They've got to feel good about themselves as well as where they work. They need to feel that the best day of their week is Monday. If you can create that environment, people just work their bloody tails off for you. And if you've got an organization of people doing that, you're going to win.

MIKE ARMSTRONG, CEO, AT&T

Motivation will almost always beat mere talent.

NORMAN R. AUGUSTINE, PRESIDENT AND CEO, MARTIN MARRIETTA

I don't think you should ever manage anything that you don't care passionately about.

DEBORAH A. COLEMAN, VICE PRESIDENT AND CFO, APPLE COMPUTERS

there is no
finish line.

NIKE MOTTO

if

people relate to the company that they work for, they will form an emotional tie to it, and buy into its dreams, they will pour their hearts into making it better.

HOWARD SCHULTZ, CHAIRMAN AND CEO, STARBUCKS

Celebrate what you want to see more of.

TOM PETERS, AUTHOR

Business is personal. People commit themselves to other people, not to organizations.

HATIM TYABJI, PRESIDENT AND CEO, VERIFONE

Nothing is so powerful

as an insight into human nature...what compulsions drive a man, what instincts dominate his action...if you know these things about a man you can touch him at the core of his being.

WILLIAM BERNBACH, COFOUNDER, DOYLE DANE BERNBACH ADVERTISING

When it comes to training and performance reviews, I think we have our priorities reversed. Shouldn't we spend more time trying to improve the performance of our stars? After all, these people account for a disproportionately large share of the work in any organization. Put another way, concentrating on the stars is a highly leveraged activity; if they get better, the impact on the group output is very large indeed.

ANDY GROVE, CHAIRMAN, INTEL

The true motivator for employees is the spirit of cooperation that comes with a shared vision.

GREG BUSTIN, SENIOR VICE PRESIDENT, TRACY-LOCK PUBLIC RELATIONS

someday

is not a day of the week.

who wants to claw their way to the middle?

The moment avoiding failure becomes your motivator; you're down the path of inactivity. You stumble only if you're moving.

ROBERTO GOIZUETA, FORMER CEO, COCA-COLA

It's not empowerment that's magic, it is accountability. Give people the responsibility and the resources to get something done. Let them understand that they will be held accountable for it, that you are expecting those results, and that they are going to share in the success. Then watch what happens.

CHARLES HEIMBOLD, CHAIRMAN AND CEO, BRISTOL-MYERS SQUIBB

My expectations of every person are far greater than their own personal expectations for themselves. I believe they all can do great things if they are put in the right environment, and given the right challenges and the right tools. So I'm very challenging. I expect a lot from people, but I expect no more of them than I expect from myself. I expect strong commitments. But I also reward people accordingly. That's how you keep people motivated. I think it's also important to recognize that success itself motivates. It's very critical that the CEO crafts plans that lead to successful performance for the corporation. You've got to be so careful about that because you can destroy the attitude of everybody in the company. Nobody wants to be part of a loser. They want to be part of a winner. They've got to see tangible, measurable results that we are winning. It's the CEO's job to make sure that happens.

BOB TILLMAN, CHAIRMAN, PRESIDENT, AND CEO, LOWE'S

PURPOSE

You have to show by example

WHAT IS IMPORTANT

I tell my VPs that if their 10-year-old has a concert, that is only going to happen one time and that concert takes precedence over an executive meeting. Again, I have to show people what I respect and I'm interested in. I think that's really important.

CAROL BARTZ, CEO, AUTODESK

do it big
or stay in bed.

ANONYMOUS

Change is not about understanding new things or having new ideas; it's about seeing old things with new eyes—from different perspectives. Change is not about reorganizing, reengineering, reinventing, recapitalizing. It's about rediscovery.

DEE HOCK, FOUNDER, VISA

What employees

are looking for is sincerity, and you don't demonstrate sincerity through making something programmatic. It has to come from the heart rather than the head.

It's virtually impossible to communicate too much. I've never heard a single employee anywhere complain that he or she is being kept **too informed.**

JIM BROADHEAD, CHAIRMAN, PRESIDENT, AND CEO, FPL GROUP

the first job of a leader is to define a vision for the organization…but without longevity of leadership you can have the vision-of-the-month club.

WARREN BENNIS, LEADERSHIP EDUCATOR, SPEAKER, AND AUTHOR

If you can connect with people

and show them that their organization cares about them first as human beings, and everything else is second to that, then you have a chance of being a great organization. If your objective is to build an institution that lasts forever, then I think that the first brick of connecting with people is connecting with them on the grounds that you care about them and the organization cares about them as human beings first. You need to find an easy way to demonstrate that the belief is real, and not just some syrupy sentiment that everybody puts in their annual report.

PAUL O'NEILL, CHAIRMAN AND CEO, ALCOA

You must be in tune with the times and prepared to **break with tradition.**

WILLIAM M. AGEE, CHAIRMAN, BENDIX

I solemnly promise and declare that every customer that comes within ten feet of me, I will smile, look them in the eye, and greet them, so help me Sam.

WAL-MART PLEDGE

if you pay attention

at every moment, you form a new relationship to time. In some magical way, by slowing down, you become more efficient, productive, and energetic, focusing without distraction directly on the task in front of you. Not only do you become immersed in the moment, you become that moment.

MICHAEL RAY, SCHOOL OF BUSINESS, STANFORD UNIVERSITY

We're not going to consume our talent or people in the sole purpose of achieving financial results. We have a higher purpose that we're committed to.

RAY GILMARTIN, CHAIRMAN, PRESIDENT, AND CEO, MERCK

When you come right down to it, the secret of having it all is loving it all.

JOYCE BROTHERS, PSYCHOLOGIST

Risk always brings its own rewards: the exhilaration of breaking through, of getting to the other side, the relief of a conflict healed, the clarity when a paradox dissolves. Whoever teaches us this is the agent of our liberation. Eventually we know deeply that the other side of every fear is freedom.

MARILYN FERGUSON, AUTHOR

work is much more fun than fun.
it's improperly called work.

TRAMMELL CROW, REAL ESTATE DEVELOPER

SUCCESS

It's important if you're successful that you

SET AN EXAMPLE

for the people who work for you in the way you conduct

your life. You know, jumping on a train rather than

jumping in a limousine or going second class rather than

first class. Little things are quite important.

RICHARD BRANSON, CHAIRMAN, THE VIRGIN GROUP

pour your heart into it.

HOWARD SCHULTZ, CHAIRMAN AND CEO, STARBUCKS

There is no scientific answer for success. You can't define it. You've simply got to live it and do it.

ANITA RODDICK, FOUNDER, BODY SHOP

we know who we are and what we do.

MICHAEL DELL, FOUNDER, CHAIRMAN, AND CEO, DELL COMPUTERS

Smell the cheese often

so that you know when it is getting old.

SPENCER JOHNSON, AUTHOR, *WHO MOVED MY CHEESE?*

I think everybody in the organization can make a contribution. And the more you can create an environment where everybody believes that, the more impact you're going to have on the overall performance of the company.

KEN LAY, CHAIRMAN AND CEO, ENRON

Honesty is just paramount. People have to trust a CEO. They've got to know he walks the talk, or she walks the talk. They've got to know the CEO believes in something besides profits. We try to foster a strong belief in the importance of the individual and the importance of our people. We think profits are important, but they're not as important as the individual.

BILL MARRIOTT, CHAIRMAN AND PRESIDENT, MARRIOTT INTERNATIONAL

success is getting what you want; happiness is wanting what you get.

ANONYMOUS

The times to be toughest are when things are going the best.

DONALD E. KEOGH, PRESIDENT, COCA-COLA

132

I can't imagine a person becoming a success who doesn't give this game of life everything he's got.

WALTER CRONKITE, TELEVISION NEWS ANCHOR

first we will be best
then we will be first.

GRANT TINKER, TELEVISION PRODUCER

If you stand up

and be counted, from time to time you may get yourself

knocked down. But remember this: A man flattened by an

opponent can get up again. A man flattened by conformity

stays down for good.

THOMAS J. WATSON, FOUNDER, IBM

I don't think success is a place or a definition, I think it's a direction. It's very important to look at how you're living your life—and it should be pointed in the right direction.

CHARLES WANG, FOUNDER, CHAIRMAN, AND CEO, COMPUTER ASSOCIATES

to lead the people,
walk behind them.

LAO-TZU, FOUNDER OF TAOISM

Leadership involves finding a parade

and getting in front of it; what is happening is that those parades are getting smaller and smaller and there are many more of them.

JOHN NAISBETT, CHAIRMAN, NAISBETT GROUP

Today, loving change, tumult, even chaos is a prerequisite for survival, let alone success.

TOM PETERS, AUTHOR

The best leaders...almost without exception and at every level, are master users of stories and symbols.

TOM PETERS, AUTHOR

What is the recipe for successful achievement? To my mind there are just four essentials: Choose a career you love...Give it the best there is in you...Seize your opportunities...And be a member of the team.

BENJAMIN F. FAIRLESS, PRESIDENT, U.S. STEEL

Among the CEOs that I know, the most successful ones have a very positive outlook. Every CEO has to be a cheerleader. At times you feel that you can list a series of disaster scenarios for your company...Still, you have to be a cheerleader at least part of the time.

RICHARD A. ZIMMERMAN, CEO, HERSHEY FOODS

To succeed, it is necessary to accept the world as it is and rise above it.

MICHAEL KORDA, EDITOR-IN-CHIEF, SIMON & SCHUSTER

self-confidence is important. confidence in others is essential.

WILLIAM SCHREYER, CEO, MERRILL LYNCH

I don't say **never** to anything.

RICHARD M. BRESSLER, CEO, BURLINGTON NORTHERN RAILROAD

WINNING

Companies that learn to

MANAGE CHANGE

are in the best position to continue to take the

risks needed to stay out in front.

MICHAEL DELL, FOUNDER AND CEO, DELL COMPUTERS

in business, the competition will bite you if you keep running, if you stand still, they will swallow you.

WILLIAM KNUDSEN, CHAIRMAN, FORD

Fantasizing, projecting yourself into a successful situation, is the most powerful means there is of achieving personal goals. That's what an athlete does when he comes onto the field to kick a field goal with three seconds on the clock, 80,000 people in the stands, and thirty million watching on TV. The athlete, like the businessman, automatically makes thousands of tiny adjustments necessary to achieve the mental picture he's forming of the success situation: a winning field goal.

LEONARD LAUDER, PRESIDENT AND CEO, ESTÉE LAUDER

thank goodness all flops aren't failures.

LILLIAN VERNON, FOUNDER, LILLIAN VERNON

As winning companies

find they must engage workers' hearts as well as their minds, this increasingly emotional aspect of business is destroying the old corporate machismo that once allowed us to keep our feelings hidden and our inner lives mysterious, even to ourselves...To the degree that individuals are successful at plumbing their depths, those people should be better off, and the companies that employ them may gain competitive advantage. In fast-shifting markets, the unexamined life becomes a liability.

"THE LEARNER WITHIN" *FORTUNE*

Nothing focuses the mind better than the constant sight of a competitor who wants to

wipe you off the map.

WAYNE CALLOWAY, CHAIRMAN, PEPSICO

Winners can tell you where they are going, what they plan to do along the way and who will be sharing the adventure with them.

DENIS WAITLEY, MOTIVATIONAL SPEAKER AND AUTHOR

nobody remembers
   who came in second.

CHARLES SCHULTZ, CARTOONIST

Too many of us are hung up on what we don't have, can't have, or won't ever have. We spend too much energy being down, when we could use that same energy—if not less of it—doing, or at least trying to do, some of the things we really want to do.

TERRY MCMILLAN, AUTHOR

you've got to do what you do well.

LOU NOTO, CHAIRMAN AND CEO, MOBIL

are you going to eat lunch or have your lunch eaten for you?

WILLIAM T. ESREY, CHAIRMAN, SPRINT

Winning is not everything, but the effort to win is.

ZIG ZIGLAR, MOTIVATIONAL SPEAKER AND AUTHOR

you cannot add to the stature of a dwarf by cutting off the legs of a giant.

BENJAMIN FAIRLESS, PRESIDENT, U.S. STEEL

The thrill, believe me, is as much in the battle as in the victory.

DAVID SARNOFF, FOUNDER, RCA

It is said that democracies that trade with one another almost never go to war. Just imagine the possibilities if individuals were to experience the same results by trading in this new, global marketplace.

JEFF SKOLL, VICE PRESIDENT, EBAY

the high-impact way
to recognize and reward employees

The Win-Wins@Work product line from Franklin Covey is the high-impact way to help managers recognize great work, congratulate, encourage, motivate, thank, or provide feedback in an instant. Maybe that's why it's generating so much excitement as one of the most innovative employee recognition programs to date.

Other Win-Wins@Work™ Products by Franklin Covey

What Counts: How Forward-Thinking Leaders Recognize and Reward Employees

Bragging Rights™ Messages

Congrats Pack™

You Rock Cards™

Win-Wins@Work Magnet

Win-Wins@Work Bookmark

For more information or to order, call Franklin Covey at 1-800-952-6839

About Franklin Covey

Franklin Covey is the world's leading time management and life leadership company. Based on proven principles, our services and products are used by more than 15 million people worldwide. We work with a wide variety of clients—Fortune 500 material—as well as smaller companies, communities, and organizations. You may know us from our world-renowned Franklin Planner or any of our books in the 7 Habits series. By the way, Franklin Covey books have sold over 15 million copies worldwide—over 1 1/2 million each year. But what you may not know about Franklin Covey is that we also offer leadership training, motivational workshops, personal coaching, audio and video tapes, and *PRIORITIES*™ magazine, just to name a few. If you want more information, see us on the web at www.franklincovey.com or visit a Franklin Covey store near you.

Franklin Covey

2200 West Parkway Boulevard

Salt Lake City, Utah 84119-2331

www.franklincovey.com

1-800-952-6839

International (801) 229-1333

Sources and Acknowledgements

Andrews, Robert. *Cassell Dictionary of Contemporary Quotations,* Cassell Wellington House, 1996.

———— *The Concise Columbia Dictionary of Quotations.* Columbia University Press, 1990.

Boone, Louis E. *Quotable Business.* Random House, 1999.

Cook, John. *The Book of Positive Quotations.* Fairview Press, 1993.

Covey, Stephen R. *Daily Reflections for Highly Effective People.* Simon & Schuster, 1994.

Eisen, Armand. *Go for the Gold.* Andrews and McMeel. 1995.

Fast Company, 1997—1999.

Feuer, Susan. *Believing in Ourselves: The Wisdom of Women.* Andrews and McMeel, 1997.

Frank, Leonard Roy. *Quotationary.* Random House, 1999.

Griffith, Joe. *Speaker's Library of Business Stories, Anecdotes, and Humor.* Prentice Hall, 1990.

Hyland, Bruce, and Merle Yost. *Reflections for Managers: A Collection of Wisdom & Inspiration from the World's Best Managers.* McGraw-Hill, 1994.

Levey, Joel, and Michelle Levey. *Living in Balance: A Dynamic Approach for Creating Harmony & Wholeness in a Chaotic World.* Conari Press, 1998.

Maggio, Rosalie. *An Impulse to Soar: Quotations by Women on Leadership.* Prentice Hall, 1998.

———— *Quotations from Women on Life.* Prentice Hall, 1997.

Maxwell, John C. *The 21 Indispensable Qualities of a Leader.* Thomas Nelson, 1999.

Nelson, Bob. *1001 Ways to Energize Employees.* Workman Publishing Company, 1997.

———— *1001 Ways to Reward Employees.* Workman Publishing Company, 1994.

Quinn, Tracy. *Quotable Women of the Twentieth Century.* William Morrow and Company, 1999.

Warner, Carolyn. *The Last Word: A Treasury of Women's Quotations.* Prentice Hall, 1992.

Zadra, Dan. *I Believe in You.* Compendium Incorporated, 1999.

————*To Your Success: Thoughts to Give Wings to Your Work and Your Dreams.* Compendium, 1997.